I0902021

My First Book of Ocean Animals

ALL ABOUT MARINE WILDLIFE FOR KIDS

GINJER L. CLARKE

ROCKRIDGE PRESS

Copyright © 2021 by Rockridge Press, Emeryville, California

No part of this publication may be reproduced, stored in a retrieval system, or transmitted in any form or by any means, electronic, mechanical, photocopying, recording, scanning, or otherwise, except as permitted under Sections 107 or 108 of the 1976 United States Copyright Act, without the prior written permission of the Publisher. Requests to the Publisher for permission should be addressed to the Permissions Department, Rockridge Press, 6005 Shellmound Street, Suite 175, Emeryville, CA 94608.

Limit of Liability/Disclaimer of Warranty: The Publisher and the author make no representations or warranties with respect to the accuracy or completeness of the contents of this work and specifically disclaim all warranties, including without limitation warranties of fitness for a particular purpose. No warranty may be created or extended by sales or promotional materials. The advice and strategies contained herein may not be suitable for every situation. This work is sold with the understanding that the Publisher is not engaged in rendering medical, legal, or other professional advice or services. If professional assistance is required, the services of a competent professional person should be sought. Neither the Publisher nor the author shall be liable for damages arising herefrom. The fact that an individual, organization, or website is referred to in this work as a citation and/or potential source of further information does not mean that the author or the Publisher endorses the information the individual, organization, or website may provide or recommendations they/it may make. Further, readers should be aware that websites listed in this work may have changed or disappeared between when this work was written and when it is read.

For general information on our other products and services or to obtain technical support, please contact our Customer Care Department within the United States at (866) 744-2665, or outside the United States at (510) 253-0500.

Rockridge Press publishes its books in a variety of electronic and print formats. Some content that appears in print may not be available in electronic books, and vice versa.

TRADEMARKS: Rockridge Press and the Rockridge Press logo are trademarks or registered trademarks of Callisto Media Inc. and/or its affiliates, in the United States and other countries, and may not be used without written permission. All other trademarks are the property of their respective owners. Rockridge Press is not associated with any product or vendor mentioned in this book.

Interior and Cover Designer: Darren Samuel
Art Producer: Janice Ackerman
Editors: Erin Nelson and Maxine Marshall
Production Editor: Sigi Nacson
Production Manager: Riley Hoffman

Hardcover ISBN: 978-1-63878-640-5 | Paperback ISBN: 978-1-64876-795-1
eBook ISBN: 978-1-63807-621-6
R0
Printed in China

For the Irwin family of Australia Zoo, who continue
to inspire me and people everywhere to love, respect, and
care for animals of every kind.

Planet Earth

The Ocean

Earth is called the blue planet. It gets this nickname because it's covered in salty water. Salty bodies of water are called oceans or seas. The biggest oceans are the Atlantic, Pacific, Indian, Arctic, and Southern Oceans.

But the oceans are not made only of water. Below the surface are underwater mountains, seagrass meadows, **kelp forests**, **coral reefs**, and more. Some parts of the ocean are so deep that they're completely dark!

At the top of the ocean, the water is a little warmer. As you dive deeper, it gets colder. In all parts of the ocean, there are lots of living creatures.

Kelp forest

Iceberg

Animals of the Sea!

An ocean animal spends most of its life in the ocean. Some animals live where the ocean meets land. Some live in the **open ocean**. Others live at the very bottom of the ocean. **Marine** animals dive, swim, flap, flip, and float in oceans all around the world. The word *marine* means "of the sea."

Penguins and seal

Dolphins near coral reef

The oceans are home to about one million different **species** of animals—from tiny **plankton** to huge whales. In this book, you will discover some of the most fascinating species. Ocean animals include marine **mammals**, marine **reptiles**, marine **invertebrates**, **fish**, and **seabirds**.

Blue whale

Whales

Whales are marine mammals. They're **warm-blooded**, like humans. Whales breathe air through blowholes on top of their heads. Most whales are giant, but they only eat tiny food. Many of the largest whales have **baleen** instead of teeth. Their massive mouths puff out to scoop up a big gulp of water. The baleen catches lots of small **krill** for the whale to eat, and the water pours back out.

The blue whale is the biggest animal in the world—it is almost as long as two semitrucks! Some whales have amazing water skills. The blue whale dives and splashes its tail out of the water. The gray whale swims straight up and down and pops up its head. The humpback whale jumps out and twists backward.

Whales talk to each other. They can squeak, rumble, or groan underwater. The male humpback whale even sings, but its songs sound like moaning or crying.

Type: marine mammal

Habitat: open ocean, near shore

Ocean: all oceans

Food: krill, plankton, shrimp, fish

Lifespan: up to 200 years

Size: 9–98 feet; 300–400,000 pounds

Gray whale

Dolphins

Dolphins are small whales with teeth. Their beak-like mouths are great for snapping up lots of fish. Porpoises are dolphin cousins, but they don't have beaks. The orca, or "killer whale," is also a type of dolphin. Dolphins can be different colors, as well as solid, striped, or spotted.

Most dolphins of the same species live together in large groups called **pods**. They're fast swimmers and they love to play! Bottlenose dolphins leap, twist, and surf in the ocean waves.

Type: marine mammal

Habitat: open ocean, near shore

Ocean: all oceans

Food: fish, squid, crabs, shellfish, starfish

Lifespan: up to 60 years

Size: 4–32 feet; 100–12,000 pounds

Spotted dolphins

Porpoise

Scientists believe dolphins are some of the smartest animals. They're also curious and social. Like whales, dolphins talk to each other, using clicks and whistles.

Dolphins don't sleep like people. They have to keep breathing while they swim, so they stay half awake. They always keep one eye open!

Type: marine mammal

Habitat: ocean edge, rocks, ice

Ocean: all oceans

Food: fish, crabs, octopus, squid, krill

Lifespan: up to 30 years

Size: 4–20 feet; 110–11,000 pounds

Sea lions

Seals and Sea Lions

Seals are sleek swimmers. They use their front and back flippers to zoom through the cold water in search of fish. Sea lions are similar to seals, but they have ears that stick out instead of earholes. Sea lions also have forward-facing flippers that help them walk on land.

Some seals, such as the harp seal, are small. The larger leopard seal has sharp teeth. The male elephant seal is huge and has a big, bumpy nose. California sea lions gather in groups of up to 1,000. It can get noisy, because sea lions bark like dogs!

Seals, sea lions, and walruses are animals called pinnipeds. Pinniped *means "fin-feet," because these animals use their fins to walk on land.*

Elephant seal

Walruses

Walruses have bodies like seals and sea lions, but they are enormous! They have whiskery beards, wrinkly skin, and elephant-like tusks. These tusks are teeth that grow up to three feet long on male walruses. Tusks are used for fighting and finding food. They are also handy tools for moving on slippery ice!

A group of walruses is called a huddle. They lie in a big pile on top of one another to warm up.

Type: marine mammal

Habitat: ocean edge, rocks, ice

Ocean: Arctic, North Atlantic, North Pacific

Food: worms, shellfish, snails, shrimp, small fish

Lifespan: about 40 years

Size: up to 12 feet; up to 4,500 pounds

Walruses

Little blue penguins

Penguins

Penguins are seabirds, but they can't fly—except underwater! These speedy swimmers use their flippers like wings. They also waddle on rocks and slide on ice. Penguins live in cold places, where they gather together for warmth. They take turns moving from the edge of the group to the middle, so everyone keeps cozy.

Type: seabird
Habitat: ocean edge, islands, rock, ice
Ocean: all southern oceans
Food: krill, fish, squid
Lifespan: up to 30 years
Size: 16–42 inches; 2–82 pounds

Emperor penguin

Like other birds, penguins lay eggs. The parent penguins take turns holding the egg and then feeding their fluffy chick. The smallest type of penguin is called the little blue penguin. The largest is the emperor penguin. The macaroni penguin has pointy yellow feathers on its head!

Adélie penguins eat lots of pink krill. They eat so much it turns their poop pink! The rocks they live on are also pinkish from their poop.

School of fish

Marine Fish

All fish have **gills** that they use to breathe in the water. Their bodies are covered in scales and they have fins for swimming.

Big fish swim alone and hunt smaller fish. The superfast swordfish stabs squid with its long snout. The ocean sunfish is the heaviest bony fish in the world. It weighs more than 2,000 pounds!

For safety, small fish swim in large groups called **schools**. But don't worry—small fish are good at hiding, too! Clown fish hide in colorful sea anemones. The leafy sea dragon blends into its surroundings by clinging to kelp.

The longest bony fish is the giant oarfish, which can grow to over 50 feet long. Its silvery, snaky body and frilly red mane make it look like a real sea monster!

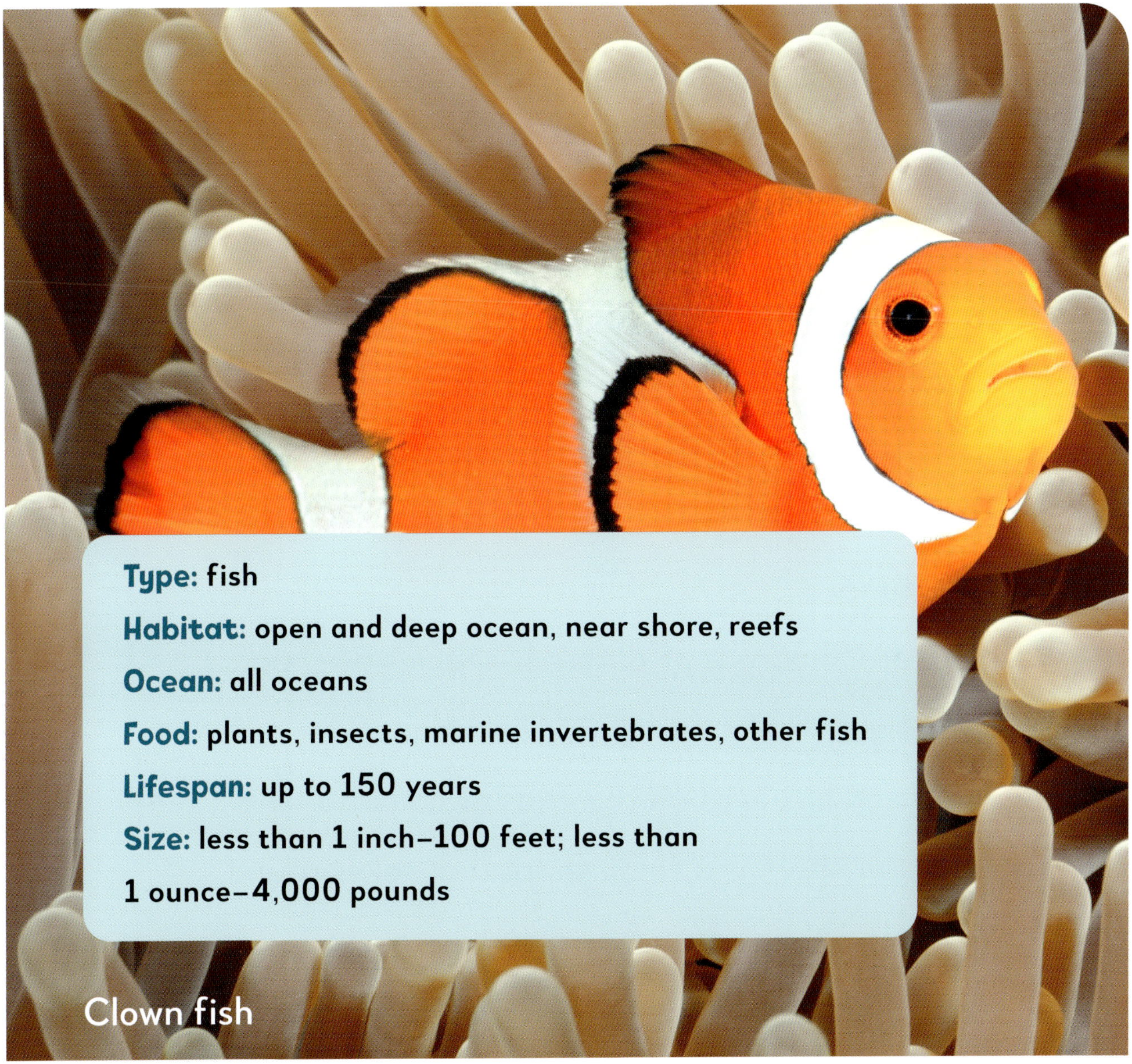

Type: fish

Habitat: open and deep ocean, near shore, reefs

Ocean: all oceans

Food: plants, insects, marine invertebrates, other fish

Lifespan: up to 150 years

Size: less than 1 inch–100 feet; less than 1 ounce–4,000 pounds

Clown fish

Sharks

Sharks are the world's largest fish, but they don't have bones. Their skeletons are made of strong, flexible **cartilage** that bends—like your ears.

The biggest shark is the whale shark. It's longer than a school bus! But it doesn't have any teeth, and it eats only tiny creatures.

There are hundreds of different species of sharks. A young tiger shark has stripes like a tiger. The hammerhead has eyes on the ends of its head. The cookiecutter shark is a small shark that takes round, cookie-shaped bites out of its **prey**!

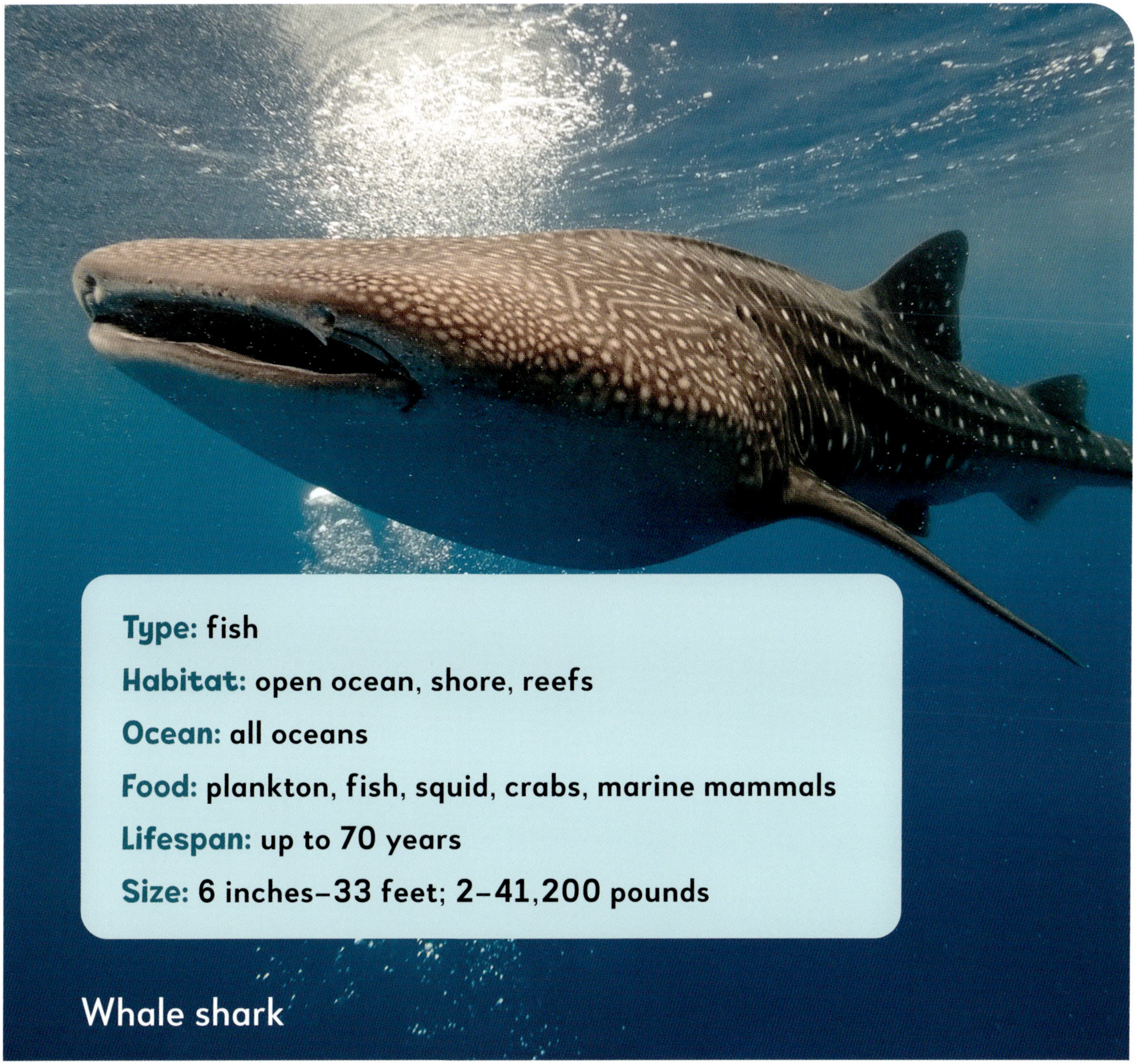

Type: fish

Habitat: open ocean, shore, reefs

Ocean: all oceans

Food: plankton, fish, squid, crabs, marine mammals

Lifespan: up to 70 years

Size: 6 inches–33 feet; 2–41,200 pounds

Whale shark

The Greenland shark is the only shark that lives in the cold Arctic Ocean. Scientists believe this shark can live to be 500 years old!

Greenland shark

Hammerhead shark

Rays

Rays are flat fish with large, winglike fins. They often hide under the sand. Some rays have sharp stingers on their tails.

The blue-spotted stingray is beautiful but deadly. The giant manta ray looks scary, but it's harmless to humans. The electric ray is small, but it can create a big shock!

Type: fish

Habitat: open ocean, near shore, ocean floor

Ocean: all oceans

Food: plankton, marine invertebrates, fish

Lifespan: up to 50 years

Size: 4 inches–23 feet; 1–3,500 pounds

Manta ray

Eels

Eels are fish with bodies like snakes. They don't have scales, and their skin is very slimy. Moray eels come in lots of colors and can be striped or spotted. These eels squeeze into tight spaces in rocky reefs with just their heads poking out. Then they pop out fast to grab a fish—surprise!

Type: fish

Habitat: open and deep ocean, reefs

Ocean: warmer oceans

Food: crabs, fish, marine invertebrates

Lifespan: up to 55 years

Size: 1–11 feet; 2–55 pounds

Green moray eel

Striped moray eel

Spotted moray eel

Sea Turtles

Like all other reptiles, marine reptiles are **cold-blooded**. They need sunshine to get warm. Sea turtles are marine reptiles. Most sea turtles have hard shells. But the leatherback turtle has a softer, rubbery shell, and it is the largest sea turtle. The green turtle is a strong but slow swimmer. The hawksbill turtle has a sharp, hooked beak.

Hawksbill turtle

Sea turtles live in the ocean all the time, except when the female turtle comes on land at night to lay hundreds of eggs in a nest. Then she returns to the sea. The tiny baby turtles hatch and then wiggle quickly over the sand and into the ocean.

Leatherback turtles are world travelers. They have been tracked swimming thousands of miles!

Type: marine reptile

Habitat: open ocean, shore, reefs

Ocean: all oceans except Arctic and Antarctic

Food: jellyfish, marine invertebrates, crabs, seagrass

Lifespan: up to 50 years

Size: 2–7 feet; 100–2,000 pounds

Hawksbill turtle

Marine Iguanas

Only one type of lizard lives in the ocean: the marine iguana! This iguana eats only one kind of food—slimy **algae**. A marine iguana dives beneath the surface. It rips algae off rocks underwater with its strong jaws. Afterward, the iguana climbs onto sunny rocks to get warm.

Type: marine reptile

Habitat: rocks and ocean edge

Ocean: Galápagos Islands in the Pacific Ocean

Food: algae

Lifespan: up to 12 years

Size: 4–5 feet; 1–3 pounds

Marine iguana

Jellyfish

Jellyfish are not fish. They are marine invertebrates. They have no bones, blood, or brains. Only box jellyfish have eyes. Jellyfish come in many different sizes. One type of box jellyfish is smaller than your fingernail. The giant Nomura's jellyfish is huge! It weighs as much as a male lion.

Type: marine invertebrate

Habitat: open ocean

Ocean: all oceans

Food: plankton, snails, shrimp, fish, squid

Lifespan: up to one year (except for the immortal jellyfish)

Size: less than 1 inch–120 feet; less than 1 ounce–200 pounds

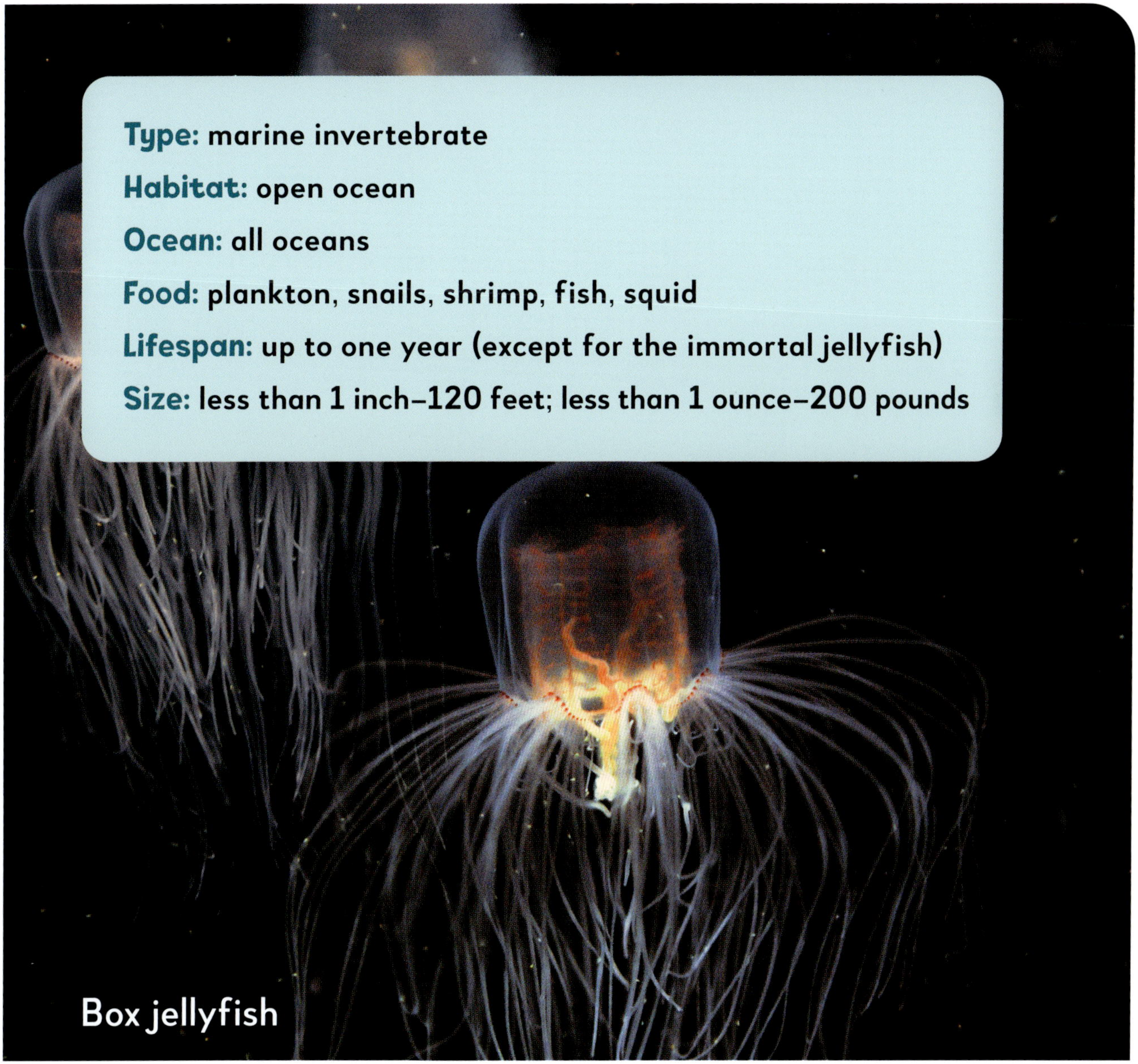

Box jellyfish

Man-of-war jellyfish

Jellyfish are mostly made of water and need water to live. Many jellyfish have stinging **tentacles**. They use these tentacles to capture prey and to protect themselves from **predators**, such as turtles and fish.

The man-of-war jellyfish lives at the top of the ocean, floating on the surface. Many other jellyfish live at the bottom of the ocean. They glow in the dark to communicate with other creatures.

Immortal *means "to live forever." The immortal jellyfish is the only animal we know of that can go from being an adult back to being a baby over and over again. It might get eaten, but it never dies of old age!*

Coral

Coral reefs look like they are made of colored rocks. But, actually, coral are living creatures with tiny tentacles. The largest coral reef is the Great Barrier Reef in Australia. It can even be seen from outer space! The shapes formed by coral can look like an elkhorn, pencil, star, fan, mushroom, or brain.

Type: marine invertebrate

Habitat: reefs, open and deep ocean

Ocean: all oceans, but reefs only in warm oceans

Food: algae, plankton

Lifespan: up to 4,000 years

Size: up to 5 inches each, but reefs can be miles wide

Coral reef

Coral reef

Brain coral

Type: marine invertebrate

Habitat: shore, rocks, open ocean

Ocean: all oceans

Food: marine invertebrates, seaweed, algae

Lifespan: up to 100 years

Size: 1 inch–12 feet; 1 ounce–44 pounds

Christmas Island red crab

Crabs

Crabs, along with lobsters and shrimp, are **crustaceans**. They have hard shells and sharp claws. Crabs come in different colors, such as the Christmas Island red crab and Atlantic blue crab. They can be teeny like the yellowline arrow crab or gigantic like the Japanese spider crab, whose legs are each five feet long!

Some crabs can change their shells. The colorful hermit crab doesn't have its own shell, so it moves into an empty snail shell. The decorator crab covers its shell and legs with seaweed, sponges, and rocks. Now it looks like part of the coral reef!

Crabs can walk forward and backward, but they mostly walk and run sideways. They are called decapods, *meaning "ten-footed," because they have eight legs and two big claws.*

Hermit crab

Octopuses

An octopus has eight limbs that are covered in suckers to grab things. It can squirt ink to escape predators and can swim backward. It can also completely change its color and shape.

An octopus can see in the dark, and it has a big brain, too. It also has a beak like a bird, but the beak is inside its head!

Type: marine invertebrate

Habitat: ocean edge, open and deep ocean

Ocean: all oceans

Food: crabs, clams, snails, fish

Lifespan: up to 5 years

Size: less than 1 inch–16 feet; less than 1 ounce–110 pounds

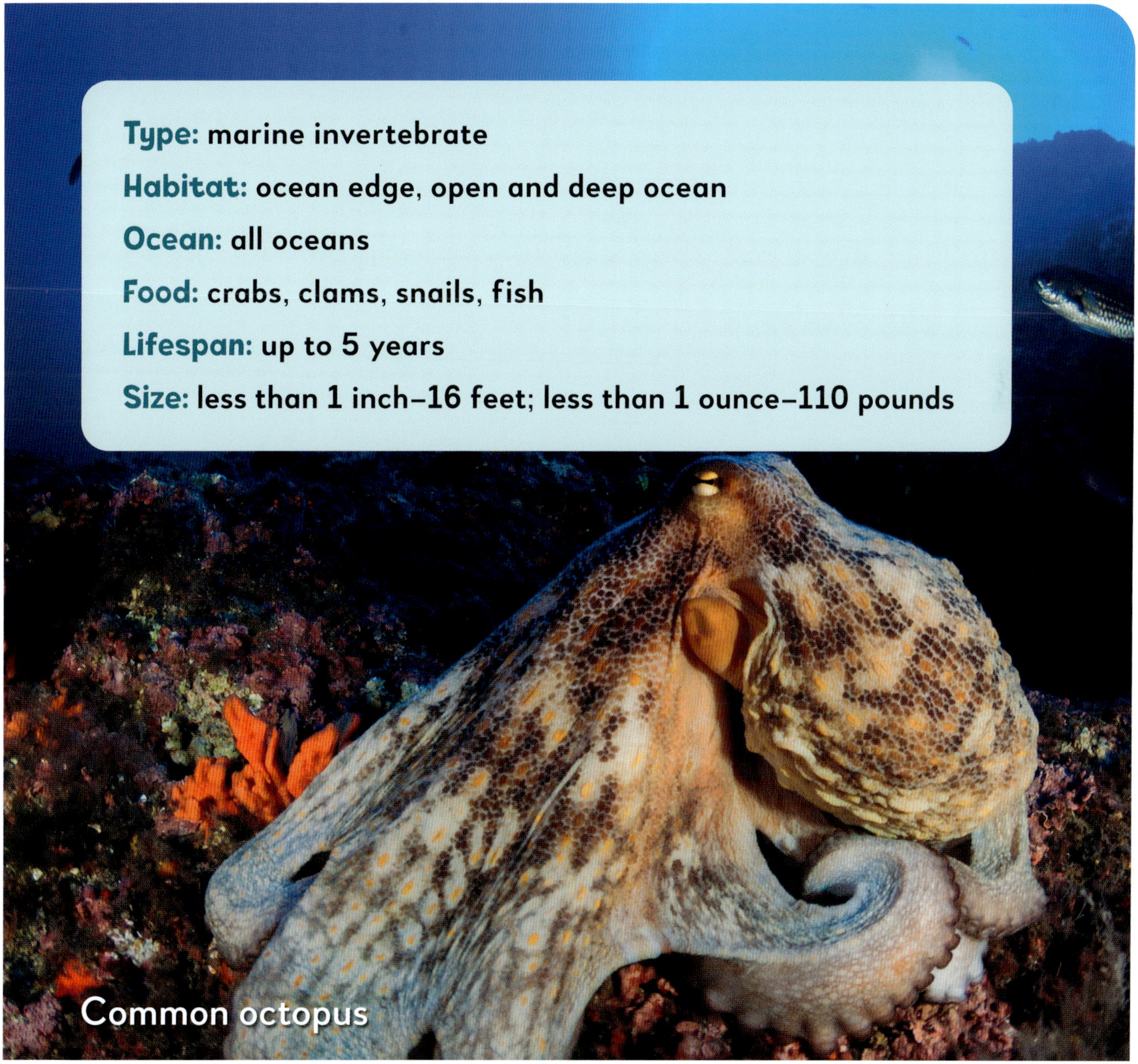

Common octopus

The giant Pacific octopus's arms reach 16 feet across. Each arm is as tall as a giraffe! The blue-ringed octopus is small but has a bite that is deadly to both animals and people who step on it.

The giant Pacific octopus has three hearts, nine brains, and blue blood!

Giant Pacific octopus

The Ocean and You

Scientists are still learning new things about our incredible oceans. Our planet is changing, and some changes, like ocean water getting warmer, can cause problems for ocean animals.

You are not an ocean creature, but you are important to the ocean. People who care about the ocean and its animals can protect it for the future. This is called ocean **conservation**.

Porcupine puffer fish

GLOSSARY

ALGAE: (AL-jee) Simple, green water plants

BALEEN: (BAY-lean) Thin bristles that some whales have instead of teeth, used to catch food and release water

CARTILAGE: (CAR-till-ej) Strong, flexible material that is not as hard as bone and is found in the bodies of some mammals and fish

COLD-BLOODED: Having a body temperature that changes when the temperature outside changes

CONSERVATION: The act of taking care of and protecting the environment

CORAL REEF: A raised area of rocky coral at or just below the ocean's surface

CRUSTACEAN: (crus-TAY-shun) A marine invertebrate such as a crab, a lobster, or a shrimp

FISH: A cold-blooded vertebrate animal with gills and fins that lives in water

GILLS: An organ, similar to lungs, that fish use to breathe in water

INVERTEBRATE: An animal without a backbone or spine

KELP FOREST: A large underwater area where brown seaweed called kelp grows in strands from the ocean floor to the surface

KRILL: Tiny shrimp-like creatures

MAMMAL: A warm-blooded vertebrate animal that has hair or fur and drinks milk when it's a baby

MARINE: Living in or produced by the sea; means "of the sea"

OPEN OCEAN: The part of the ocean away from land

PLANKTON: Very tiny floating water creatures

POD: A group of marine animals, especially dolphins and whales

PREDATOR: An animal that hunts and kills other animals for food

PREY: An animal that is hunted and killed by another animal for food

REPTILE: A cold-blooded vertebrate animal with scaly skin that lays eggs on land

SCHOOL: A large group of fish or marine mammals

SEABIRD: A bird that lives mainly in the sea or ocean, or on shore

SPECIES: A group of animals or plants that are related and are similar to one another

TENTACLES: (TEN-tuh-kuls) Thin limbs that an animal uses to grab, move, and sense things around it

VERTEBRATE: An animal with a backbone or spine

WARM-BLOODED: Having a body temperature that stays the same all the time

ABOUT THE AUTHOR

Ginjer L. Clarke is the author of more than 30 nonfiction children's books about animals. She loves researching cool science stuff and writing in her pajamas, but she also enjoys giving author presentations at schools, libraries, and conferences. When she's not reading or writing, she's probably dancing, hiking, or kayaking. Visit her online at GinjerClarkeBooks.com.

IMAGE CREDITS

Cover photography: © sans_patrie/istock

Interior photography: Alamy Stock Photo: p. 5: ©Image Professionals GmbH, p. 48: ©Stephen Frink Collection, p. 57: ©Alexey Stiop; istock by Getty Images: iv: deliormanli, p. 2: ©Andrew Stowe, p. 3: ©posteriori, p. 6: ©ultramarinfoto, p. 8: ©gremlin, p. 11: ©Gerald Corsi, p. 13: ©tswinner, p. 14: ©Vanhop, p. 16: ©slowmotiongli, p. 19: ©burroblando, p. 21: © thirtydry, p. 22: ©slowmotiongli, p. 24: ©Grafissimo, p.35: ©crisod, p. 37: ©marcduf, 38: ©atese, p. 39: ©Joe Belanger, 41: ©Rainer von Brandis, p. 51: ©IBorisoff, p. 52: ©ltos, p. 63: ©sans_patrie; shutterstock: p. 26: © Keiki, p. 29: ©cbpix, p. 31: ©Krzysztof Odziomek, p. 32: ©Dotted Yeti, p. 33: ©Alex Rush, p. 43: © Yann Hubert, p. 45: ©Natursports, p. 47: ©Gino Santa Maria, p. 53: ©Francisco J. Ramos Gallego, p. 54: ©John A. Anderson, p. 59: © Antonio Martin, 61: ©Naoto Shinkai

Author photo courtesy of Jess Lucia Photography